OWJC
8/11

CATS SET V
The Designer Cats

CHAUSIE CATS

Jill C. Wheeler
ABDO Publishing Company

visit us at
www.abdopublishing.com

Published by ABDO Publishing Company, 8000 West 78th Street, Edina, Minnesota 55439. Copyright © 2011 by Abdo Consulting Group, Inc. International copyrights reserved in all countries. No part of this book may be reproduced in any form without written permission from the publisher. The Checkerboard Library™ is a trademark and logo of ABDO Publishing Company.

Printed in the United States of America, North Mankato, Minnesota.
092010
012011

 PRINTED ON RECYCLED PAPER

Cover Photo: Photo by Helmi Flick
Interior Photos: Photo by Helmi Flick pp. 5, 9, 11, 13, 15, 16, 17, 18, 21;
    Photolibrary pp. 7, 19

Series Coordinator: Heidi M.D. Elston
Editors: Heidi M.D. Elston, BreAnn Rumsch
Cover & Interior Design: Neil Klinepier
Production Layout: Jaime Martens

Library of Congress Cataloging-in-Publication Data

Wheeler, Jill C., 1964-
  Chausie cats / Jill C. Wheeler.
      p. cm. -- (Cats. Set V, Designer cats)
  Includes bibliographical references and index.
  ISBN 978-1-60453-729-1 (alk. paper)
  1. Chausie cat--Juvenile literature. I. Title.
  SF449.C47W44 2010
  636.8--dc22
                                            2009021145

Thinking about a Designer Cat?
Some communities have laws that regulate hybrid animal ownership. Be sure to check with your local authorities before buying a hybrid kitten.

CONTENTS

FABULOUS FELINES

Scientists believe today's house cats are **descendants** of wildcats. The wildcats helped control **rodent** populations in human villages. Over time, people began to value the cats as companions.

There are 37 cat species in the world today. All cats are members of the family **Felidae**. This family includes big cats such as lions, tigers, and leopards. Domestic, or tame, cats also belong to this family.

Today's domestic cat lovers can choose from 30 to 40 different **breeds**. Yet for some people, that is still not enough choice. The newest trend is designer cats. Designer cats are bred to look like a wildcat but have the personality of a domestic cat.

There are more than 500 million house cats in the world today. That makes house cats the largest cat species.

One popular designer cat is the chausie. It is a mix of the jungle cat and either a domestic shorthair or an Abyssinian. The name *chausie* comes from the jungle cat's scientific name, *Felis chaus*.

JUNGLE CATS

Jungle cats are native to Africa and Asia. They range from the Nile Valley north to Turkey and the Caspian Sea. And, they live eastward through South Asia as far as Vietnam. These wildcats are found in wetlands and river valleys.

The first record of the jungle cat was found in Egypt. **Archaeologists** discovered jungle cat mummies in ancient Egyptian tombs. This suggests Egyptians greatly valued the cats. They used them to hunt wild waterfowl.

Jungle cats are strong swimmers and excellent hunters. They eat ground-dwelling birds, **rodents**, and other small animals. Sometimes they eat the young of larger animals, too.

The jungle cat has long legs and black tufts of hair on the ears. Its slender body is 20 to 30 inches (51 to 76 cm) long. Its tail adds another 10 to 11 inches (25 to 28 cm). Male jungle cats weigh 25 to 35 pounds (11 to 16 kg). Females weigh 15 to 25 pounds (7 to 11 kg).

People have long admired jungle cats for their beauty and athletic ability.

DOMESTIC CATS

The domestic shorthair cat is called the British shorthair in Great Britain. In North America, it is known as the American shorthair.

This sturdy cat has a round head, round eyes, and ears with rounded tips. Usually, the coat is short. Silver, brown, blue, and red are common colors for this **breed**.

Abyssinians are among the oldest cat breeds. Many people believe they are from Egypt. Abyssinians were imported into North America from Great Britain in the 1900s.

The Abyssinian is a curious, active, and affectionate cat. It has a slender body, large ears, and almond-shaped eyes. This domestic cat also has short, **dense** fur. And, it has a ticked coat that features hair banded with two or more colors.

The British shorthair weighs 9 to 18 pounds (4 to 8 kg).

The Abyssinian weighs 9 to 17 pounds (4 to 8 kg).

The American shorthair weighs 8 to 15 pounds (4 to 7 kg).

In the Mix

People first began **breeding** chausie cats in the late 1960s and early 1970s. At that time, many people liked the idea of having a jungle cat for a pet. However, jungle cats are wild animals. They rarely make good pets.

Some breeders thought mixing jungle cats with house cats might be the answer. They hoped to create a cat that looked like a jungle cat. But, they wanted it to have the personality of a domestic cat.

Early breeders crossed many different house cats with jungle cats to create chausies. Breeders eventually settled on two domestic breeds, the Abyssinian and the domestic shorthair.

Chausies make
excellent companions.

CHAUSIE CATS

Cat lovers worldwide think chausies are some of the most beautiful designer cats. Many chausies look a lot like jungle cats.

Chausies have small feet and large ears. Some have small tufts of hair at the top of their ears. These tame cats have gold, yellow, hazel, or light green eyes. Some even have a three-quarter tail. That feature comes from their jungle cat relatives.

These beautiful designer cats are excellent hunters, runners, and jumpers. Their long, lean, muscular bodies reflect those talents. For example, chausie cats have slightly longer back legs than front legs. This helps them run and jump.

Many chausie breeders prefer the three-quarter tail. This type of tail has fewer vertebrae than a full-length tail.

BEHAVIOR

Chausie owners say their pets are good-natured, loyal, and affectionate. In fact, some owners say their chausies are a lot like dogs. These owners have trained their chausies to walk on a leash and play fetch.

Like their wild ancestors, chausies are very active. They sleep less than other house cats. And, they are more active in the evening.

Chausies are smart animals. They can easily become bored, which can lead to trouble! Owners should give their cat plenty of attention and toys. They may even need to provide a **feline** playmate for their cat.

This lovable cat is
always ready to play!

COATS & COLORS

Chausie coats feature short to medium length fur. The fur is **dense** and a bit coarse. Regular brushing helps keep a chausie's coat in good condition. An occasional bath will also help the coat stay healthy.

Chausie **breeders** recognize three colors of chausie cats. These are solid black, brown ticked tabby, and black grizzled ticked tabby. All of these colors are found in jungle cats.

Black grizzled ticked tabby

The brown ticked tabby exhibits a sandy gray to reddish gold coat. Each individual hair has two to three bands of dark color. This cat's face, legs, and

Brown ticked tabby

tail have dark markings. There should also be bold stripes on the upper inside of both front legs.

The black grizzled ticked tabby's coat is slightly different. Each hair has light and dark bands of color with a dark tip.

SIZES

A cat's size depends on how big or small its parents are. The jungle cat is large compared with most common house cats. So, the chausie is a larger domestic cat.

Chausies weigh between 15 and 30 pounds (7 and 14 kg). They stand 14 to 18 inches (36 to 46 cm) tall at the shoulders.

Male chausies are bigger than females.

Most smaller female cats give birth to kittens about two months after mating. Larger wildcats carry their young for about four months. Kittens are born completely helpless.

Though chausie cats are large, they are also very graceful. Many people say they look like the natural athletes they are.

CARE

Caring for a chausie takes time and energy. It is not always easy keeping up with such an active cat. They do not sit still for long. They do not like spending a lot of time alone. And, they do not do well in small places. Owners must offer their chausies plenty of time and space to play actively.

Like all cats, chausies require regular care from a veterinarian. Even indoor cats need **vaccines**. And, they should be **spayed** or **neutered** at the proper age.

Most owners train their chausies to use a **litter box**. This can be a challenge, however. Some chausies may not be very far removed from their wild jungle cat relatives. Those chausies may not want to use a litter box.

Chausies need good **nutrition** to maintain a long, healthy life. All chausies need fresh water and a high-quality commercial cat food. With proper love and attention, chausies should live for 12 to 16 years.

Like many cat breeds, chausies love heights. They jump gracefully and quietly to high locations.

GLOSSARY

archaeologist (ahr-kee-AH-luh-jihst) - one who studies the remains of people and activities from ancient times.

breed - a group of animals sharing the same ancestors and appearance. A breeder is a person who raises animals. Raising animals is often called breeding them.

dense - thick or compact.

descendant - a person or an animal that comes from a particular ancestor or group of ancestors.

Felidae (FEHL-uh-dee) - the scientific Latin name for the cat family. Members of this family are called felids. They include domestic cats, lions, tigers, leopards, jaguars, cougars, wildcats, lynx, and cheetahs.

feline - of, relating to, or affecting cats or the cat family.

litter box - a box filled with cat litter, which is similar to sand. Cats use litter boxes to dispose of their waste.

neuter (NOO-tuhr) - to remove a male animal's reproductive organs.

nutrition - that which promotes growth, provides energy, repairs body tissues, and maintains life.

rodent - any of several related animals that have large front teeth for gnawing. Common rodents include mice, squirrels, and beavers.

spay - to remove a female animal's reproductive organs.

vaccine (vak-SEEN) - a shot given to animals or humans to prevent them from getting an illness or a disease.

WEB SITES

To learn more about chausie cats, visit ABDO Publishing Company online. Web sites about chausie cats are featured on our Book Links page. These links are routinely monitored and updated to provide the most current information available.

www.abdopublishing.com

INDEX